KOALAS

Sandie Lee Books

Koalas

The Koala is not a bear. It is a marsupial, like a kangaroo. It got its name from early settlers that thought this fluffy mammal looked like a bear. The word "koala" is an aboriginal word meaning "no drink." There are 2 species of the koala; the northern and southern. Its closest relative is the wombat. Millions of years ago there were koala-like animals. In fact, there was around 12 different species, but they are now all extinct.

Where in the World?

Did you know that koalas only live in Australia? These woolly mammals live among the tall eucalypt forests in and around the Australian islands. They also love the low woodland areas where the eucalyptus trees are found. The koala calls these specific Australian states home; Queensland, North South Wales, Victoria and South Australia.

The Body of a Koala

Did you know koalas have a pouch? They also have big fluffy ears, small eyes, a thick grey coat to keep warm and strong powerful legs. The koala's nose is quite large for its face and is leathery in appearance. It uses its long claws to climb trees and its sharp teeth to tear into the eucalyptus plant.

The Size of the Koala

Did you know there are two sizes of the koala? The northern koala is smaller and can weigh up to 16 pounds. The southern koala is larger and weighs in at 30 pounds. The koalas in the southern regions also have a thicker coat, as the weather is cooler there.

What a Koala Eats

Did you know the koala's main diet is eucalyptus? Koalas only eat the leaves and tender shoots of the eucalyptus tree. Even though there are different species of this plant, the koala knows which ones it likes to dine on. The koala rarely drinks water because it gets all it needs from this plant.

The Koala's Special Ability

Did you know the koala smells like cough drops? Because the koala eats only the eucalyptus plant, its fur smells minty. This is because the eucalyptus plant is naturally minty. You may have tried eucalyptus yourself. This ingredient can be found in cough drops and medicine. I guess the koala will never get a sore throat!

The Koala as a Predator

Did you know the koala is not a predator? This peaceful marsupial does not hunt or kill anything. It lives its life among the eucalyptus forests and only eats this plant. The koala rarely even fights with another koala. To mark its territory, it simply leaves its scent on its "home trees."

The Koala as Prey

Did you know the koala is hunted by many predators? The koala is hunted by dingos, owls, large lizards and people. When the koala comes down from the trees, wild dingos and lizards will prey on them. Man has also been hunting the koala for years for its meat and fur.

Koala Talk

Did you know koalas can communicate? Males use a loud bellowing sound to let other koalas know where it is and to defend its territory. Mother koalas will make soft humming, grunts and clicking noises to talk to their babies. All koalas when frightened make a loud shrieking sound, as well as shaking.

The Koala Mom

Did you know the mother koala is only pregnant for about a month? A female koala is ready to have a baby when she is about 4 years-old. She will find a mate, then leave to have her baby. The female koala has a built-in baby carrier, it is her pouch!

The Baby Koala

Did you know a baby koala is called a 'Joey?'
The joey is born without fur and ears and is
blind. It is only about the size of a jellybean.
The baby koala must find its way from the birth
canal to its mother's pouch. Here it will nurse on
milk.

A Special Food

Did you know the eucalyptus plant is poisonous? The baby koala nurses milk from its mom until it is 6 months old. At this time a special food called, 'pap' is supplied to the joey. This food comes from the mother's intestines and has an enzyme that keeps the koala safe when it eats the eucalyptus plant.

Koalas at Rest

Did you know koalas are kind of lazy? The koala spends about 18 hours of its day resting, sleeping and eating high up in the eucalyptus trees. It rarely comes down from the trees. To get from one tree to the other, it will leap using its powerful back legs.

Koalas at Play

Did you know koalas like to play? Baby koalas will play among the trees with each other. One joey will be much older than the other. They use play to practice jumping and leaping. The koala is also a great swimmer and will take to the water to cool off and to play.

Life of a Koala

Did you know the koala can live to be around 18 years old? Since the habitat of the koala is shrinking and they have many predators, some of the koalas do not live past being a baby. The koala's natural habitat is now being protected and many zoos have taken in abandoned or injured koalas.

Quiz

Question 1: The koala is not a bear, so what is it?

Answer 1: A marsupial

Question 2: Where does the baby koala stay?

Answer 2: In its mother's pouch

Question 3: What special item does the koala smell like?

Answer 3: Cough drops. This is because of the eucalyptus plant it eats.

Question 4: What does the koala hunt?

Answer 4: Nothing

Question 5: What is the special food the mom koala gives her baby to protect it from the poison in the eucalyptus?

Answer 5: Pap. This comes from her intestines.

Thank you for checking out another addition from Sandie Lee Books! Make sure to check out Amazon.com for many other great titles.